DISCOVER
OAHU

The Gathering Place

Text by
STU DAWRS

Photography by
ANN CECIL

This page, clockwise from top left:
*Hula girl dancing at sunset in Waikīkī.
An intricate Hawaiian quilt (Hawaii
State flag design). Catamaran off
Waikīkī. Beach stroll at sunset. Fisher-
man off Waimānalo coastline. Hawai-
ian ipu (gourds) with kukui nut leis on
tapa cloth. Local boy playing guitar on
the beach. Yellow Hibiscus.*
*Opposite, clockwise from top left:
Best friends. Sunrise over Chinaman's
Hat, Kāne'ohe Bay. Leis draped over
statue of King Kamehameha. Island
beauty. Hawaiian quilt making. Conch
shell blower. Pink and yellow plumeria.
Shadows of palms along Waimānalo
Beach. Lū'au food! Page 1: Orchid lei
on beach. A delicate wild 'Ilima flower.*

CONTENTS

E KOMO MAI

WELCOME!

THERE'S A STANDARD RIDDLE about O'ahu that goes something like this: "O'ahu's nickname is 'The Gathering Place'; its flower is the *'ilima*; what is its bird?"

One glance at the skyline from nearly anywhere on the island's south shore and the answer is immediately apparent: "The steel crane."

Only the third largest of the Hawaiian Islands at 607 square miles, O'ahu's population of some 870,000 comprises almost 80 percent of the entire island chain—with a great concentration (nearly 380,000) in the Honolulu area. The main campus of the University of Hawai'i, with its 18,000 full-time students, is located in Mānoa Valley, on the slopes above Waikīkī. The per capita population density of Makiki, an area just east of downtown, is comparable to that of Manhattan. Honolulu is truly a metropolis in the middle of the Pacific. Even so, there is a certain innocence to all of it, as illustrated by the unique tendency of *kama'āina* (a native-born or longtime resident) toward understatement—most locals simply refer to the Honolulu area as "Town."

And Town is only part of the story of O'ahu. "Country"—that is, O'ahu's famed north shore—is a Mecca not only for surfers from around the world seeking what are generally considered to be the best (and largest) waves on the planet but also for townies look-

ing to escape the urban landscape for an area closer to the Hawai'i of old. The island's west shore—which, in another ode to linguistic functionality, is usually just referred to as "West Side"—is home to a large Hawaiian population and a smoother, quieter lifestyle.

Even from the heart of downtown Honolulu, solitude is 10 minutes away in virtually any direction. The hills above town are crisscrossed with a network of picturesque hiking trails, most of which eventually lead more experienced hikers to the cliff's edge of the Ko'olau Mountains and panoramic views of lush windward O'ahu.

Yes, O'ahu has been built upon. Even so, it doesn't take much searching to find what might be referred to as the "true Hawai'i." On the north shore, just around the corner from the famed surf break of Waimea Bay and across Kamehameha Highway from the prime summer snorkeling site known as Shark's Cove, stands a Foodland shopping center. Here also, a mile or so up the winding Pūpūkea Road, stands the remains of the ancient Pu'uomahuka *heiau*. Dedicated to Kū, the god of war, Pu'uomahuka was a *heiau po'okanaka*—that is, a site where human sacrifices were offered to the god. Measuring 575 feet long and 170 feet wide, the *heiau* has the largest area of any on

Preceding pages: Snorkeling with fish at Hanauma Bay.
Above: The green Ko'olau Mountains from the windward side.
Background: A bird's eye view above
Waikīkī Beach and Honolulu.

Above: Colorful spinnakers, Ala Wai Boat Harbor. Left: pro surfer Gerry Lopez, Pipeline Master's Surf contest, North shore. Below: Waves at Yokohama Bay, Leeward side. Opposite top: Koʻolau Mountains. Center, left to right: Hiker on the Maunawili Trail. Hikers on the Maunawili Trail, windward side. Couple and rainbow on ʻEhukai Beach, North shore. Bottom: Puʻu O Mahuka Heiau, North shore.

Above, clockwise from top: *Rainbow and palms. The Mission Houses Museum. Bananas and produce, Chinatown. Meat market and shoppers, Chinatown. Bottom left: Trolley in Chinatown. Opposite top: 'Iolani Palace. Bottom: Pineapple patterns in Kunia on the 'Ewa Plain.*

O'ahu, and legend has it that its dedicatory fires at one time burned hot enough to warm Kaua'i.

Such is the paradox of O'ahu—an island that encompasses everything cosmopolitan *and* rural. Virtually every day, in the heart of an urban landscape like Honolulu, one sees rainbows arcing over the lush valleys that hem in the downtown area. A walk through the downtown proper yields historic sites that range from 'Iolani Palace (the only royal residence in the United States) to the Mission House Museum (the first Congregationalist missionary settlement on O'ahu) to the historic Chinatown district (twice razed by fires near the turn of the 20th century and now a bustling

home to markets that sell everything from traditional medicinal herbs to souvenirs for visitors). A drive from town through the central plains of Oʻahu provides a window into Hawaiʻi's changing economy, where sugar and pineapple once reigned king and where other, smaller agricultural ventures are being developed to replace the all-but-dead large-scale plantations.

Standing in the midst of all of this is Oʻahu's incredibly varied population. In the past, some have referred to Hawaiʻi as "The Melting Pot of the Pacific," a designation that is grossly unfair to the many distinct ethnic groups whose cultures are a unique yet integral part of Hawaiʻi's social landscape. At various times through-

HĀNAU

BIRTH

ACCORDING TO THE STORY that has come down through many centuries, Oʻahu is the result of a tryst between a man and a goddess. The short version holds that Papa the earth-mother—who, with Wakea the sky-father was responsible for the creation of the entire universe—had only just returned from a visit to Tahiti when she learned that Wakea had been unfaithful, having fathered a series of island children with the moon goddess Hina. Out of spite, Papa took up with a handsome young lover named Lua. To make a long and colorful story a bit dryer, the end result of their union was the island of Oʻahu.

Though slightly more pragmatic, the scientific explanation of Oʻahu's birth is nonetheless just as fascinating. Like all of the more than 130 islands, islets and shoals that make up the Hawaiian Island chain, Oʻahu is believed to be the creation of a single "hot spot" in the earth's mantle. Beginning with the submerged Emperor Seamounts on the northwestern end of the 1,600-mile chain, the earth's crust is believed to have very gradually drifted to the northwest across this hot spot. As it did so, over the course of several million years, the various islands in the chain were formed, until the spot reached its present point beneath the island of Hawaiʻi, where volcanic eruptions continue to this day.

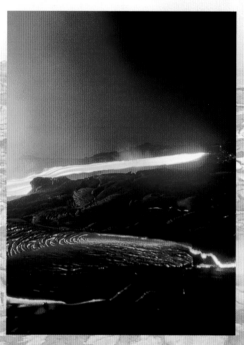

Like the island of Maui, Oʻahu is the product of volcanic activity by two large shield volcanoes. Estimated to have first broken the sea's surface some 9-10 million years ago, lava flowing from both mountains eventually joined to form Oʻahu's large and fertile central plain. Known as the Leilehua Plateau, this large plain is six miles across at its widest point and runs from Waialua on the island's north shore to ʻEwa, the area just west of Pearl Harbor on the south shore. Today, due to the forces of erosion working over many eons, the long extinct volcanoes have lost the gradual shield-like shapes for which they are named. They now appear as two separate but roughly parallel mountain ranges, punctuated by numerous peaks, cathedral-shaped valleys and high, jagged cliffs known by the Hawaiian name of *pali*.

The elder of the two ranges, the Waiʻanae mountains (part of which—mount Kaʻala—is the highest point on the island at 4,020 feet), separate the drier west Oʻahu coast from the Leilehua Plateau and the north shore. The younger, lusher Koʻolau range separates the south shore and urban Honolulu from windward Oʻahu— which, like the windward side of all islands, receives the majority of the rain blowing in off the ocean.

Of the six main Hawaiian islands, Oʻahu is second only to Kauaʻi in age, and therefore erosion has played

Above: Hot yellow lava. Background: Kamoamoa Black Sand Beach lava flow.
Opposite top: Aerial view, Waiʻanae Mountain range, looking down over leeward Oʻahu.
Bottom: Dramatic ridges of the Koʻolau Mountains,
Kāneʻohe side of the mountains.

Moore's belief that huge landslides (similar to the one that would occur at Washington State's Mount St. Helens in 1980, though on a much larger scale) played as important a part as erosion in the shaping of at least some of the major land forms in the Hawaiian Islands, including the Nuʻuanu Pali.

It wasn't until 1983 that Moore would get a boost for his theory from an unlikely source. That year, president Ronald Reagan claimed sovereignty for the United States over all seabed resources within a 230-mile zone surrounding the United States, which, of course, includes Hawaiʻi. To assess the nature of these resources, the U.S. Geological Survey began an extensive mapping of the Hawaiian ridge—the 1,364-mile long, 372-mile wide, 507,000-square mile perch upon which the entire Hawaiian chain sits. What they came across was extraordinary. Debris on the sea floor indicated more than 68 major landslides measuring 12 miles or more in length between Midway Island to the northwest and the island of Hawaiʻi. Off of Kauaʻi's northern coast, known as Nā Pali, scientists found debris 87 miles offshore that suggested a 62-mile wide avalanche was responsible for carving out much of that jagged coastline some 5 million years ago.

On Oʻahu, according to the theory, this took place on a much grander scale. The cliffs rising up behind the windward towns of Kāneʻohe and Kailua are believed to be the eroded back wall of an ancient vol-

Opposite: *Golf on the 16th fairway, Ko'olau Golf Course, windward O'ahu.* Left: *Mist over the top ridges of the Ko'olaus.* Below: *The Ko'olaus from the Windward side.*

canic caldera, the other half of which literally broke off and tumbled into the sea. Proponents of the Nu'uanu Slide say there could be no other explanation for stone blocks up to 19 miles across and 11 miles wide that have been found as far as 30 miles offshore. This explanation means the slide would have been more than 1,000 times larger than that at Mount St. Helens. If this theory is correct, scientists say, it could also account for such anomalies as coral deposits which have been found at elevations of more than 1,000 feet on the Island of Moloka'i. A major slide on the island of Hawai'i's Kona coast about 100,000 years ago is thought to have created a tidal wave so large that it is barely imaginable—a wall of water over 1,000 feet tall.

*Scenes at Hanauma Bay, a
marine life conservation district.*

Another major volcanic feature of Oʻahu is the famed Hanauma Bay, on the island's southeastern shore near Koko Head. Once a coastal crater, the erosive force of ocean waves pounding on its southern rim eventually wore a large section away, creating the scenic bay that is now a marine sanctuary and prime snorkeling destination.

Whether one chooses to believe that Oʻahu's birth was the result of a union of the gods or a wonder of the natural world, it's safe to say that it was a drawn out and tumultuous birth—one that has left a distinctive and beautiful creation.

Left: *Aerial view—Waikīkī, Ala Wai Canal, Diamond Head.*
Below: *Royal Hawaiian Hotel.*
Opposite top: *Afternoon around the Moana Hotel's Banyan Court and Beach Bar.*
Bottom: *Visitors, palms, Waikīkī Beach and Diamond Head.*

which, when completed in the early 1920s, was used to drain the area. Soil dredged up during the construction of the canal was used as landfill—and greater Waikīkī was born. Once the Royal Hawaiian Hotel was completed in the late 1920s, on the former site of the royal beach house, Waikīkī was well on its way to becoming an exclusive area for the super rich. Many arrived on steamships to spend entire seasons in the hotel.

It wasn't until some 40 years later that Waikīkī would begin to lose some of its air of exclusivity, when the playground for movie stars and millionaires was barricaded, barb-wired and turned into an R&R (rest and recreation) area for GIs during World War II. These soldiers, a far cry from Waikīkī's more chic ten-

ants, would eventually return to their homes throughout the United States with tales of an island paradise. Combined with the advent of the jumbo jet and with radio and film versions of "paradise," the GI tales would lead to a construction boom. Beginning just before the 1959 statehood vote, the boom would continue through the 1970s.

Today, with area residents, workers in the visitor industry and tourists combining for an average daily population of over 100,000, Waikīkī is considered to be one of the most densely populated spots on earth. Still, with all the hustle and bustle of Waikīkī's main thoroughfares, solitude can be found. Kapiʻolani Park, just east of Waikīkī proper, is a shady oasis, its 140 acres providing plenty of space for a family picnic or an afternoon of kite flying. Likewise, though Waikīkī Beach proper can get crowded, a quarter-mile stroll leads to beaches that are relatively empty—and generally frequented more by kamaʻāina (local) families who live in the area.

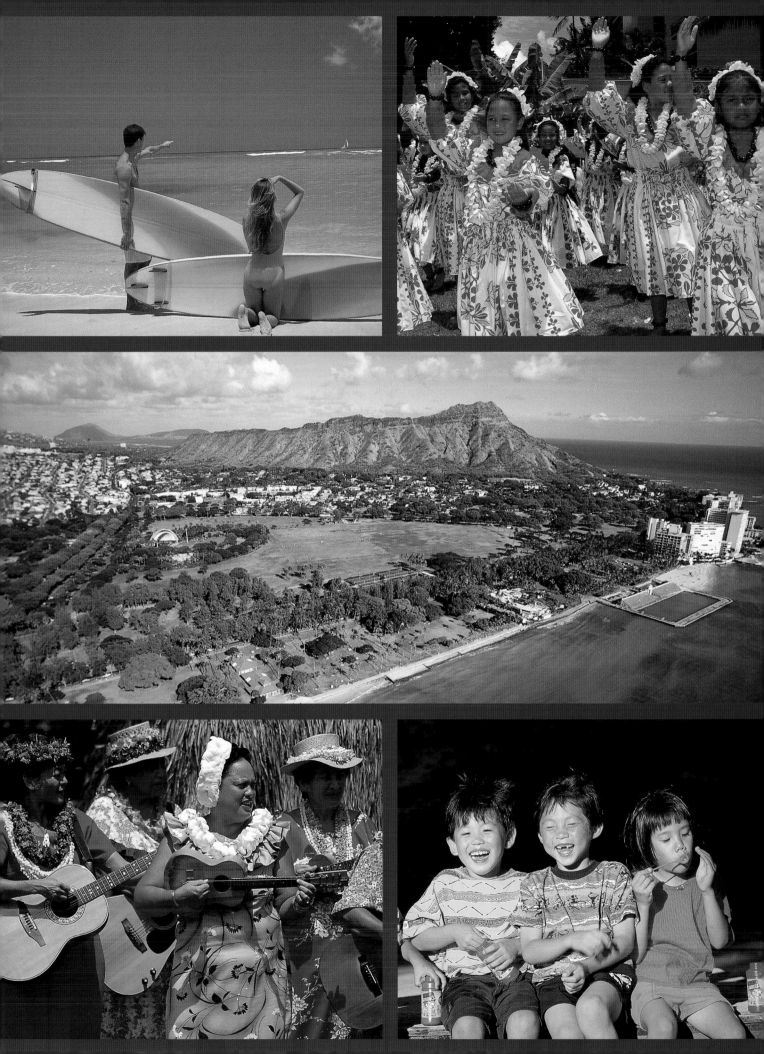

Opposite, top: *Couple with surfboards on beach near Diamond Head. Keiki hula dancers.* Center: *Aerial view of Kapi'olani Park, Diamond Head.* Bottom: *Dancers from the Kodak Hula Show. Island keiki (children) at play.*
This page, clockwise from top: *Kite festival, Kapi'olani Park. Mahimahi exhibit at Waikīkī Aquarium. Kodak Hula Show. 'Ukulele instruction.*

WAIKIKI

Preceding pages: Moon rising over Waikīkī and Magic Island. This page, top row: Duke Kahanamoku Beach, Hilton Hawaiian Village. Surfer at sunset. Kayaking at Waikīkī. This row: Bright outrigger canoe. Duke Kahanamoku statue. Below: Fire dancer. Couple shopping in Waikīkī. Diamond Head view. Hula at sunset.

Clockwise from top left:
Waikīkī lifeguard advising
Japanese tourists on safety.
Hula dancer at sunset. Palms,
sand, sea and sun in Waikīkī.
Looking down over Waikīkī
Beach. Surfboards, Waikīkī.
Hula dancers of Na Mea
Hula O Kahikinaokalalani. Sail-
boat and sunset off Waikīkī.
Center: Old style Hawaiian
musical trio, The Islanders.

Traveling further eastward, one comes almost immediately upon Diamond Head, the 760-foot-tall crater which was formed by volcanic activity late in Oahu's geological history, some 350,000 years ago. So named because a group of sailors once mistook volcanic calcite crystals for diamonds, Diamond Head's true name is Lē'ahi—which translates literally as "the head of the *ahi*." Legend has it that Hi'iaka, a sister of the volcano goddess Pele, named the crater after its resemblance to the blunt profile of an *ahi* (yellowfin tuna).

At one time, the western slopes of Diamond Head housed a *heiau* dedicated to the war-god Kū. Today, the crater itself is home to a National Guard depot. Those looking for a quick hike can walk an easy trail up the inside of the crater to an abandoned army pillbox over-looking Waikīkī and much of southeast Oahu. During the months of November through February, whale spouts can often be seen from this vantage point.

Still further eastward lie the volcanic outcroppings of Koko Head (whose crater houses a little-known but beautiful arboretum) and Hanauma Bay. Because the bay is officially designated as a fish sanctuary, it is a prime destination for snorkelers looking for a close-up glimpse of Hawai'i's various reef inhabitants.

Though some claim that Waikīkī's commercial air has tarnished some of its original magic, the area still has a charm (and excitement) that is undeniable. With the help of a little imagination (and perhaps a Mai Tai at any number of beach-front hangouts), it's not hard to find oneself in the Waikīkī of yore—in a place where fun, sun and romance still rule the day.

Opposite page: *Hiker resting and enjoying the view high atop Diamond Head.* Above: *Aerial view of Black Point and the Kāhala district.* Right: *Koko Head and the East O'ahu coastline.* Pages 36–37: *Twilight over Waikīkī, Diamond Head and Honolulu.*

KA LOKO I'A
ANCIENT HAWAIIAN FISHPONDS

FISH BEING one of the main staples of the Hawaiian diet, *ka loko i'a*—the fishpond—served not only as an ingenious method of harvesting fish from streams and bays, but also as an invaluable spiritual and cultural center for ancient Hawaiians. Though only a handful of functioning fishponds remain, at one time it is estimated that there were at least 488 freshwater, brackish and saltwater *loko i'a* throughout the Hawaiian islands (178 on O'ahu, 138 on Hawai'i, 74 on Moloka'i, 50 on Kaua'i, 44 on Maui and 4 on Lana'i).

To understand both the importance and eventual demise of the fishponds in Hawaiian life, one must first understand the concept of the *ahupua'a*. This was a land division that stretched from the uplands to the ocean and was marked at its boundaries by a mound or heap of stones (*ahu*) crowned with the image of a pig (*pua'a*), or by an altar upon which a pig or other tribute was laid as tax to the ruling chief.

Under the system of the *ahupua'a*, each community was guaranteed everything needed for subsistence: fruits and vegetables, wild boars to be hunted, medicinal plants and building materials from the upper elevations; the starchy staple food *taro* from the flatter

coastal areas that could be well irrigated by freshwater streams; and on the very edge of the *ahupua'a*, the saltwater fishpond. It was used as a simple yet ingenious aquaculture farm for the cultivation of fish and edible seaweed. Often, in the mid-elevations, freshwater fishponds were combined with irrigation systems for *taro*, pulling water off streams and through the *lo'i* (terraced *taro* fields) before looping the now nutrient-dense water back into the lowland fishponds. This created a closed system that guaranteed little water was wasted.

There was a variety of designs for freshwater, brackish and saltwater fishponds. The most common was the *loko kuapā*—saltwater or brackish ponds with sides that faced the sea and were made up of an uninterrupted rock or coral wall arcing out between two anchor points on the shore. Placed at certain strategic points in the stone wall were *mākāhā*—openings with a grate made of sticks spaced in such a way that small bait fish and water could pass through while any fish larger than half an inch in thickness were trapped inside.

Because ancient Hawaiians held a strong belief in the connection between humans, the gods and nature, fish-

Above: Morning light over Kāne'ohe Bay and Kahalu'u fishpond.
Background and opposite: Looking out to Chinaman's Hat
over the Kahalu'u fishpond.

For those that have a hard time finding "the real Hawai'i," this area is full of its remnants, in terms of both the physical and the legendary. Unlike Hono-

lulu's crowded streets, this region is lush and green. In older times, the area encasing Mōli'i was part of the *ahupua'a* of Hakipu'u. At the time, this *ahupua'a* was given over to *kāhuna* (priests), a tradition that was honored at Hakipu'u through the time of Kamehameha I. The chiefs Kahahana, Kahekili, Kalanikūpule and Kamehameha each in turn ceded the land to their respective *kāhuna*. It is perhaps because of this that the area is steeped in legend.

Hakipu'u was once the home of Kaha'i, who was said to have traveled to Samoa and brought back the first *'ulu* (breadfruit) tree to Hawai'i. It is also said that Kaupē, the dog demigod, often assumed that shape in the clouds above Hakipu'u. At certain times of day, particularly early morning or late evening, he would lead fishermen into a narrow spot of the valley and then attack them. Perhaps, when traveling through this area, it's a good idea to keep an eye on the road and one on the sky.

Above: *He'eia fishpond.*
Left: *'Ulu or breadfruit. Oppo-*
site: *Looking down over the*
Kahalu'u fishpond.

timeline and a metaphor for what transpired between Captain James Cook's first landfall in 1778 and the 1959 vote that led to Hawai'i's statehood.

Though Cook's arrival signaled the beginning of a new and challenging era for Hawai'i, the real significance of his chancing upon Hawai'i would only begin to show with another set of arrivals some 40 years later. In 1819, American ships caught a whale off the coast of the island of Hawai'i—the first to be caught in the islands; and in 1820, the first of the American Protestant missionaries arrived in the Kingdom.

Significantly, Kamehameha I, the warrior-chief who had unified all of the islands under his rule and had staunchly resisted any attempts to supplant traditional Hawaiian religious practices with any form of Christianity, died on May 8, 1819. The death of Hawai'i's first king came at a time when the old religion was no

Lili'uokalani, on January 17, 1893. In July of 1898, in part due to the United States' increasing presence in the Pacific via the Spanish-American War, Hawai'i was annexed. On August 12 of that year, amid cheers from the annexationists and the tears of many native Hawaiians, the flag of Hawai'i was brought down from its position over 'Iolani Palace, cut into small strips, and distributed throughout the gathered crowd as a memento of the day.

A little more than 60 years later, on August 21, 1959, Hawaii would become a member of the United States. In a vote mandated by the United Nations that was meant to determine the will of the native people, voters were given the choice of remaining annexed to the United States or becoming the newest state in the union. The end result being that Hawai'i, as a member of the United States, would be removed from the UN list of "non self-governing nations" (nations that were scheduled to be decolonized) and returned to self-rule

Left, above: *A magenta sunset glow over Aloha Tower.* Below: *Hula dancers at a celebration.*

Opposite, bottom left: *Statue of Kamehameha I, the first king to unify all of the islands.*

pox and leprosy. A side effect of this loss was the need to import outside laborers to work the cane fields—a process that began in 1852 with the first boatload of Chinese laborers. It would eventually include workers from Japan, Portugal, the Philippines and Europe.

Eventually, sugar interests would also lead to the forcible overthrow of the Hawaiian Monarchy. Though for a time Hawai'i enjoyed a reciprocity treaty with the United States that allowed sugar to be exported to America without tariff, in 1890 the United States replaced its sugar tariff policy with a bounty that was paid for sugar grown in the United States. Hawaiian sugar had thus lost its advantage. The industry was plunged into a depression that fueled a growing annexationist movement among the sugar growers and other non-Hawaiians who were frustrated with a lack of voice in the Hawaiian government.

This movement would eventually lead to a U.S.-backed revolt and overthrow of the reigning monarch,

under the UN charter. The vote was for statehood. However, because U.S. military personnel residing on bases in Hawai'i were allowed to vote and no option for self-governance was presented on the ballot, many Hawaiian sovereignty activists today claim that this process was at the very least flawed—and quite possibly illegal.

Today, the effects of these events are readily apparent in all aspects of Honolulu life. One need only walk three blocks west of 'Iolani Palace to see how this has played out. From the 'Iolani Palace grounds (now faced by the State Capitol building), one passes directly into the heart of Honolulu's banking district; from there, directly into the historic Chinatown area....

The Gathering Place is now truly that—gathered in this three-block area, one finds faces from every part of the globe and every social stratum—a multi-ethnic, multi-cultural society afloat in the middle of the Pacific Ocean.

Right, top to bottom: *Tamarind Square, downtown Honolulu. Tasting spicy soup in Chinatown. "Catch of the Day." Chinatown* scene. *Chinese New Year goodies for sale. Kawaiaha'o Church.* Below: *King Kamehameha statue.*

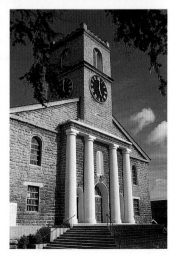

Right: *The Bishop Museum.*
Below: *Inside the Bishop Museum, with the great whale.*
Opposite page, top: *The Honolulu Academy of Arts.* Bottom: *Queen Emma Summer Palace in Nuʻuanu Valley.*
Pages 54–55: *Sunset glow over Aloha Tower Marketplace.*

THE DAY OF INFAMY

THE ATTACK ON PEARL HARBOR

IN THE ANNALS of naval warfare, December 7, 1941 will be remembered not only as the day of the greatest single defeat in United States' maritime history, but also as the day that marked the end of the age of the battleship and the dawn of the aircraft carrier. In human terms, the remembrance is much simpler. The date marks one of the greatest single tragedies in the history of Hawai'i, the United States and, for that matter, the world. Relative to the overall losses suffered on all sides during World War II, the casualties related to Japan's attack on Pearl Harbor become a minor footnote—but a visit to Pearl Harbor's Arizona Memorial drives home the very real human loss associated with war, in a way that very few sites in the United States can.

The attack on Pearl Harbor and the United States' entrance into the war was actually more than a decade in the making. This was in part the result of deteriorating relations between the United States and Japan over the security of southeast Asia in general and Japan's presence in China in particular. In essence, it began when extremists in the Japanese army invaded China's northernmost province of Manchuria, in defiance of Japan's own government policy. Though clearly worried, neither the United States nor any other country with interests in the area was willing at the time to commit military force to aid China.

Over the ensuing years, with the advent of war in Europe, Japan's alignment with Nazi Germany and its expansionist moves into the Pacific, the United States and Japan were both increasingly forced into positions that made war inevitable. By the summer of 1941, Japan was facing an embargo of U.S. oil and the United States was up against the threat of Japan's further advances into the western Pacific. Although both countries maintained the appearance of negotiating, it was clear that neither could back down without severe loss of national prestige. Japan, at this point, had already decided to go to war.

On November 26, 1941, an attack fleet of 33 ships departed northern Japan, heading across a route far north of the normal shipping lanes to Hawai'i. The fleet crossed some 4,000 miles of ocean undetected to reach a point 230 miles north of O'ahu. At 6:00 a.m. on December 7, six aircraft carriers launched the first of two waves (a total of 350 fighters, bombers and torpedo carriers) toward the unsuspecting island. Those two waves would be more devastating than any tsunami.

While the United States considered an attack against Hawai'i entirely possible, it was nonetheless almost totally unprepared for what was to happen. At Pearl Harbor, the 130 vessels of the U.S. Pacific Fleet were quietly berthed, with seven of the fleet's nine battleships moored along "Battleship Row." Since the main concern of the armed forces was saboteurs, the

Above: Above the Arizona Memorial in Pearl Harbor.
Background and opposite: Visitors entering
the Arizona Memorial.

COUNTRY

KA'ENA TO KAIWI

Dropping Down out of O'ahu's central plain, surrounded by pineapple fields and with an unbroken view of the island's north shore, it is easy to see why this area is so simply known as "Country." In truth, the view is at once so empty and breathtaking that one is left at a loss for a more eloquent description.

Traveling along the north coast eastward from Ka'ena Point, O'ahu's northwestern tip, up around the north shore and down to the island's southeastern-facing Kaiwi coast-line, one finds a diversity of people and place that is nothing short of amazing. It is all a startling contrast to the island's urban south shore.

At the point where the Wai'anae mountains finally drop down to the sea to separate the island's north and west shores, is Ka'ena, an ecologi-cally sensitive area containing a variety of rare and endangered native plants. Ka'ena is said to be named for a male relative who accompanied the fire goddess Pele on her journey from Kahiki (Tahiti) to Hawai'i. Once virtually denuded of all veg-etation and overrun by recreation vehicles, Ka'ena is a conservation success story. Now designated a Natural Area Reserve and overseen by state environmental organizations, the point's sand dunes have begun the process of regeneration.

Though hot and dry—"Ka'ena" literally translates as "the heat"—the area is a fine spot for a day hike. Meandering trails wind over two miles through the low vegetation and out to a small lighthouse on the point proper. During the winter, the reefs off Ka'ena are home to some of the largest and most unruly surf in the world—bigger even than the surf the famed Waimea Bay and for the most part deemed unridable by surfers except for a few legendary attempts. But it's a breathtaking sight and not hard to understand why Ka'ena's desolate and beautiful tip is traditionally considered to be a "jumping-off point" for souls of the dead making their final departure.

Moving east through rural Moku-lē'ia, one comes quickly to historic Hale'iwa town. Though a bypass road exists to ease traffic conges-tion through the two-lane town, Hale'iwa is not to be missed. With Hale'iwa's Ali'i Beach Park marking the beginning of the famed strip of surfing areas that ends five or so miles further north at Sunset Beach, the town has a character unique to the islands.

Lying at the northern edge of the fertile Leilehua Plateau, Hale'iwa began life as an agricultural town. Today, in essence, it's a surf town. This is especially true between the months of October and February, when strong swells bring touring professional surfers and hordes of water-borne nomads on their unending

Above: *Colorful shave ice, a local treat.*
Background and opposite: *Waimea Bay,*
on O'ahu's north shore.

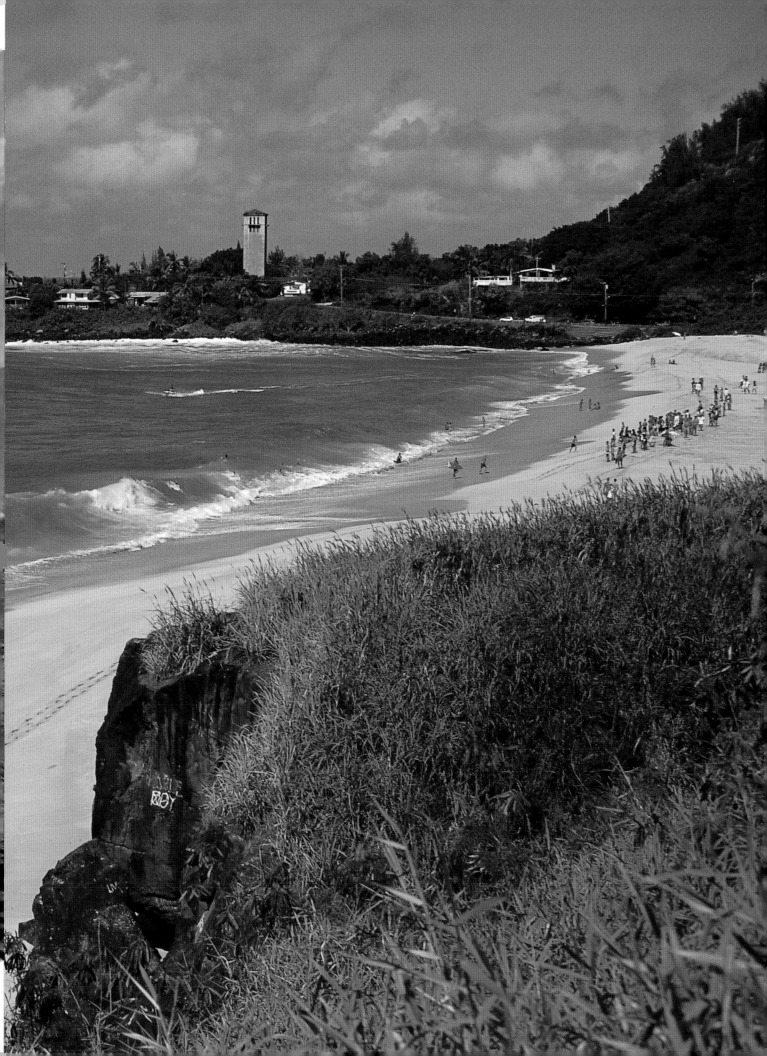

quest for the perfect wave. Haleʻiwa, and the north shore in general, take on the air of both an international sporting event and a circus, with young men and women arriving from every point on the globe for the sole purpose of testing themselves in the world's most challenging waves, Haleʻiwa's short run of boutiques, cafes, country stores and (of course) surf shops makes it the perfect people-watching destination.

Opposite top: *Road through Haleʻiwa town.* Bottom: *Surfboards for sale in Haleʻiwa.* Above: *A funky shop, Haleʻiwa.*

Right: *Haleʻiwa scenes: Surf shop. Surfer crossing sign. Eating shave ice. Aoki's shave ice store. Surfboards and duds for sale.*

Beyond Haleʻiwa, past an area that still clings tenaciously to its rural roots, the Kamehameha Highway eventually leads to the three most storied breaks in surfing history: Waimea Bay, ʻEhukai (a.k.a. the Banzai Pipeline) and Paumalū (better known as Sunset Beach). On a glass-smooth day during the off-season, it's hard to imagine the immense force that winter storms can wrack upon these beaches. In the summer months, sailboats often anchor in Waimea's scenic cove while children play on the sand at ʻEhukai and frolic in the tiny waves lapping the beach at Sunset.

However, once the first winter swell is kicked up by storms in the area of Alaska's Aleutian Islands, the ocean here is off-limits to all but the most seasoned ocean goers. The swells at Waimea can reach heights

Past Sunset, the Kamehameha Highway skirts Kahuku Point, the northern end of the Koʻolau Mountains and the separation point between the north shore and the lush windward side of the island. Like all islands, the windward area receives the majority of the island's rain. Clouds heavy with water picked up off the ocean are blown ashore and eventually forced to unload their cargo before passing over the Koʻolau range.

Once past Kahuku's fallow cane fields and shrimp farms, the road winds through the largely Mormon town of Lāʻie (home of Brigham Young University's Hawaiʻi campus). Further along, into the areas of higher rainfall, an overhanging tropical forest creates a canopy to shade the highway, occasionally opening out to provide views of calm coastal waters and deep valleys carved by heavy annual rainfall.

Opposite page, clockwise from top left: *Kahuku sign. Bananas growing on a tree. Visitor at a fruit stand. Island fruits for sale. Kahuku Sugar Mill. Samoan entertainer, Polynesian Cultural Center. Center: Maori dancers, Polynesian Cultural Center. Above: Mālaekahana State Park. Below: Weekenders at Pounder's Beach.*

Opposite, clockwise from top:
*Ka'a'awa Beach and Kualoa
Ridge. Horseback riding through
Ka'a'awa Valley. Kualoa Ridge
framing Waikāne Valley. Punalu'u
Art Gallery. Center: Charter
fishing boat, He'eia Kea Pier.
This page, clockwise from top:
Volleyball game. Ha'iku Gardens.
Valley of the Temples. Kāne'ohe
Bay in early morning light.*

Left, top to bottom: *Catamarans on beach at Lanikai. Eating shave ice. Picnic at Bellows Beach.* Above: *Windsurfers, Kailua Beach.* Opposite page,

top: *Shoreline fishing from Bellows Beach, with the twin islands, the Mokuluas, behind.* Bottom: *Waimānalo Beach.*

Past the long expanse of Kāne'ohe Bay, the highway eventually leads through scenic Kailua town (O'ahu's second largest city, with a population approaching 37,000) and on to one of the island's most beautiful beaches—Waimānalo. A far cry from Waikīkī's crowded beach, Waimānalo seems to stretch endlessly, its crystalline sand and gentle waves framed by whispering stands of ironwood trees. The people here are also a far cry from either Waikīkī's hustle or the north shore's global merry-go-round. With a population that is largely native Hawaiian and mixed-ethnicity families that have been in the area for generations, Waimānalo retains the palpable feel of what it means to grow up and live in paradise. There is a sense of calm and quiet here.

But the highway winds on, climbing up and over Makapu'u point—home of a picturesque lighthouse and a prime area for whale watching in the winter and early spring. Then it's down to the Kaiwi coastline— its dry and rocky coastal areas echoing those found on the opposite end of the island, at Ka'ena. From coastal desert to tropical rain forest and back again—and in the space of little more than an hour's drive. O'ahu is an island of many faces.

Opposite page, top to bottom:
*Dolphins in flight, Sea Life Park.
Sunrise at Makapu'u. Rocky
lava shoreline at Makapu'u.*
Above: *Rock formations over-
looking Makapu'u Beach and
Rabbit Island.* Left: *Shoreline
beneath Koko Head Crater
and the coastal road around
the eastern side of O'ahu.*
Right: *Boogie board surfer at
Sandy Beach, between Koko
Head and Makapu'u point.*

WILD WEST?

THE WAI'ANAE COAST

PICK UP most guidebooks to O'ahu and there is little mention of the West Side, except for the occasional veiled warnings about theft or bodily harm. These warnings tend to keep most visitors away from O'ahu's dry leeward coast—or even aware of its existence. More the loss for them. The area *can* be intimidating to outsiders who don't approach it with a sense of respect for those who live here. But the coastal stretch from Kahe Point Beach Park northward to the end of the paved road just south of Ka'ena Point runs through a piece of O'ahu that is unlike any other.

There's an aura surrounding the Wai'anae coast that no doubt springs in part from its history. It was here that the demigod Maui—always the mix of prankster and benefactor—came to steal fire for humans from a group of crafty mud hens who served as its keeper. It was here that, once Kamehameha had vanquished the armies of O'ahu's chief Kalanikupule, the conquered O'ahuan's came to live. (The leeward coast of all islands being generally arid, Wai'anae was not particularly desirable to the invaders.) During this period a special school was established by exiled *kāhuna* at Pōka'i Bay, located near the center of modern Wai'anae, to preserve the folklore of their O'ahu homeland.

Today, Pōka'i is a boat harbor berthing a small fleet of locally-owned fishing boats. (The name Wai'anae, incidentally, points to its heritage as a fishing community: *wai* means water; *anae* is a type of large mullet.) Though struggling economically, the leeward coast still manages to maintain both a regal spirit and a sense of community pride. As example, in an experiment that would be possible in few other communities, a unique aquaculture program was undertaken here recently. Much like the days of the *ahupua'a* system, in which neighboring families shared the duties of farming, hunting and fishing, modern Wai'anae families now share in the farming of fish in small backyard ponds. Once the fish are large enough for market, they are distributed among the various families. The simple concept of sharing that underlies this program points directly to the heart of this coast. It's this air of self-sufficiency and *'ohana* (family) that sets Wai'anae apart from the rest of O'ahu in both geography and spirit—and perhaps what also makes it intimidating to those whose perspective has been shaped by a less personal life in the city.

Above: Mākua Valley, on the far west side of the island, near the end of the road.
Background and opposite: Surf and surfers on the west side of the island
at Kea'au Beach County Park.

Left: *Looking back toward Mākua Valley and the Wai'anae Mountains along the west side's rocky lava shoreline.* Above: *Football practice in the Wai'anae Valley near Pōka'i Bay.* Below: *Surf and waves, Yokohama Bay.*

THE ISLAND OF OPPOSITES

O'AHU IS A PARADOX. Its population bulges at one coastal seam while another is virtually deserted; its green craggy valleys stand as mute testament to the effects of eons worth of erosion even as its southern shore gleams with steel and resounds with the sound of honking car horns. Ancient fishponds and *heiau* are bordered by a highway named after a warrior-king; the royal palace faces off with the State Capitol building.

Yet somehow in the midst of these opposites a harmony is achieved. Between the palace and the capitol stands a statue of Hawai'i's last monarch, Lili'uokalani. Her bronze neck is draped daily with fresh leis;

in her upturned hand a fresh flower rests—and behind her, four lanes of traffic happily come to a halt to let a pedestrian cross against the oncoming rush. The aloha spirit is as strong here as it is anywhere. It's in the rain blowing in off the windward coast and dropping into the watershed of the Ko'olau Mountains, and it's in the rainbows forming nearly every afternoon in the mist dusting the upper reaches of the valleys above downtown Honolulu.

Most of all, it's in the people who have made their lives here at The Gathering Place, surrounded by miles of blue Pacific Ocean, and yet never truly alone....

Clockwise from top: *Statue of Queen Lili'uokalani. Hula dancers Kekai and Shenri. Hawaiian couple. Lei maker Molly. Young hula girl. Sisters Jenna and Kawai.* Center: *Young working professional couple.* Background: *High rises of downtown Honolulu and Queen Lili'uokalani.* Opposite, center: *A plaque in front of Washington Place, the Governor's mansion, commemorating Queen Lili'uokalani and "Aloha 'Oe," the song she wrote.* Page 84, top: *Smiling hula dancer.* Bottom: *Young dancers celebrate Lei Day.*

82